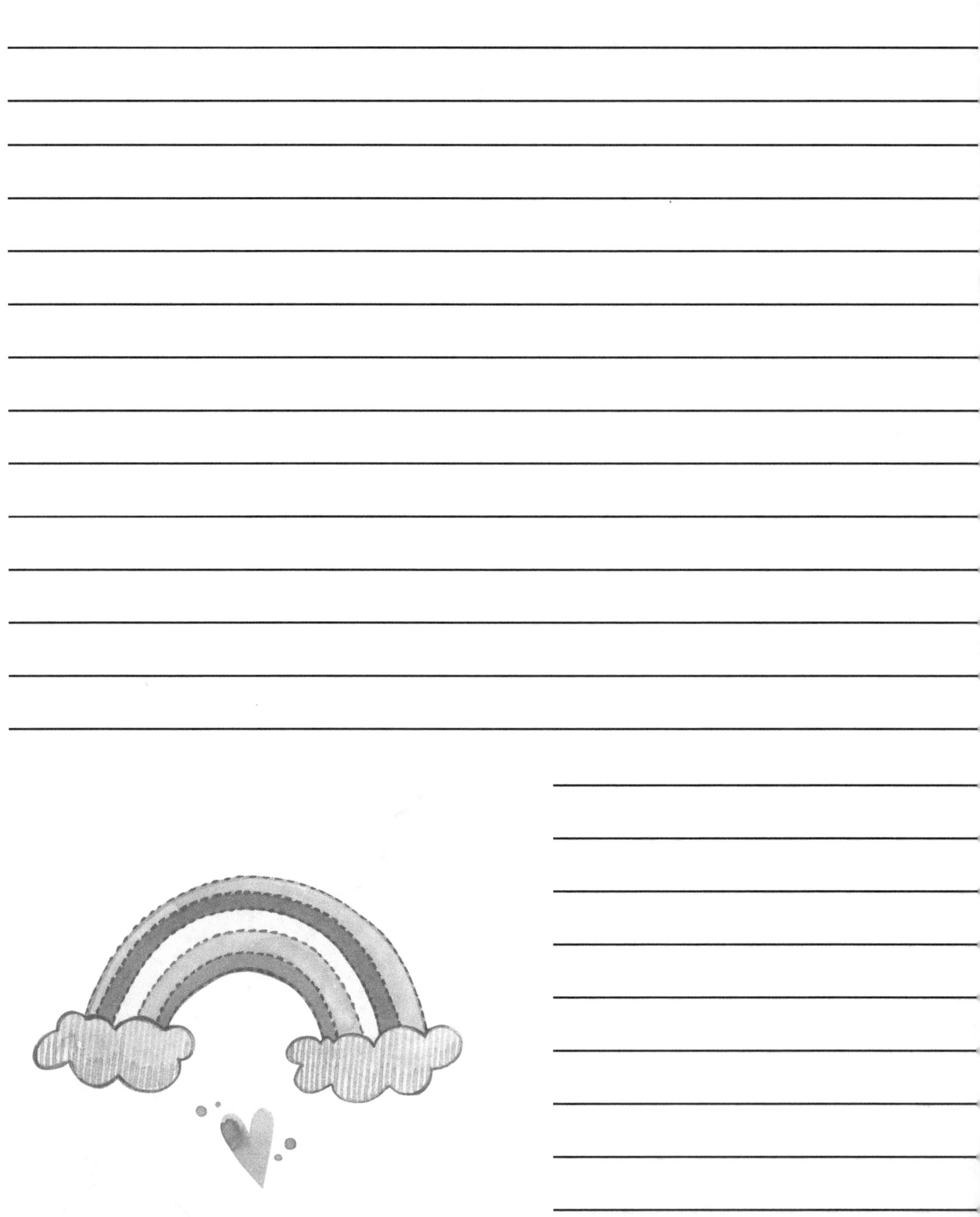

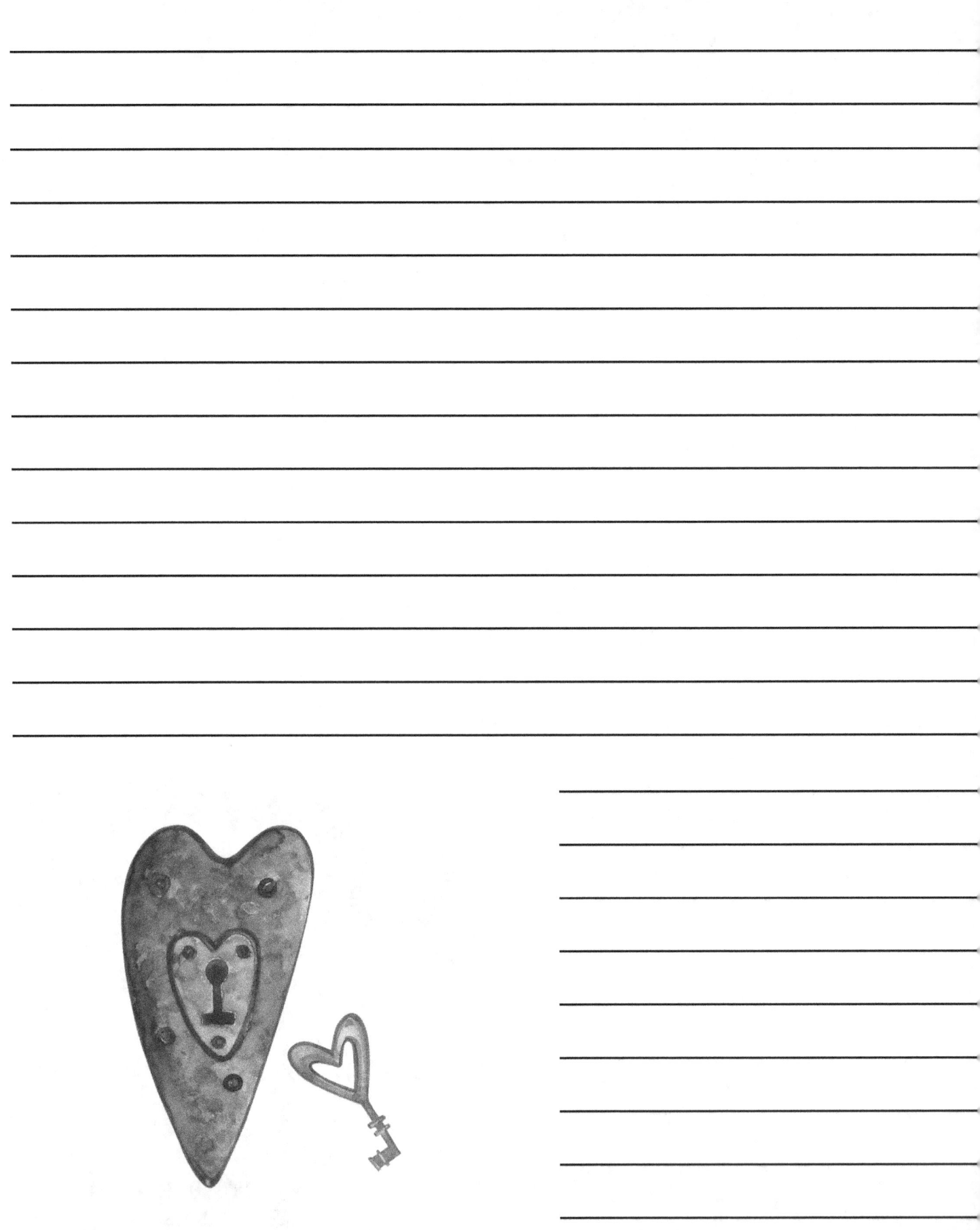

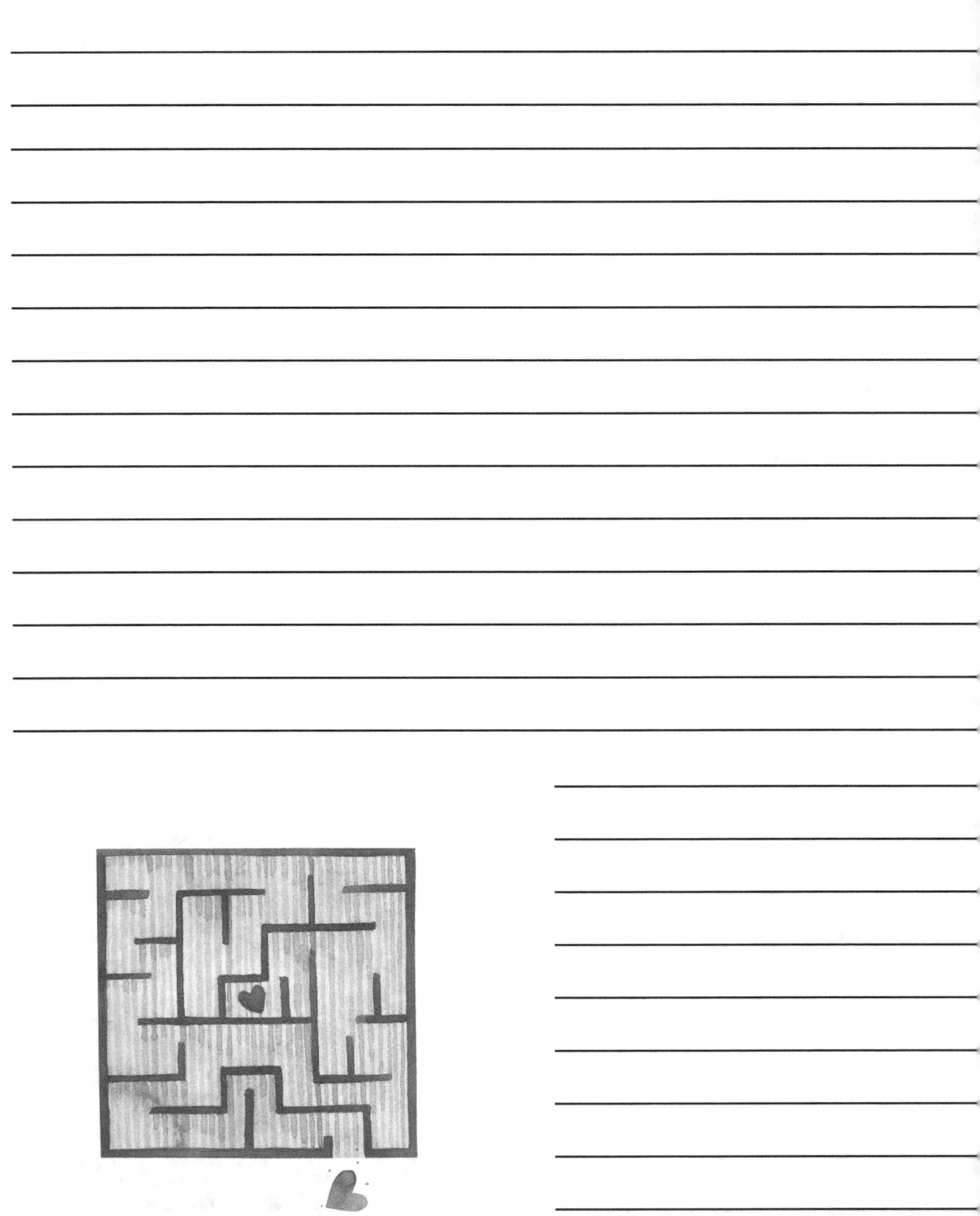

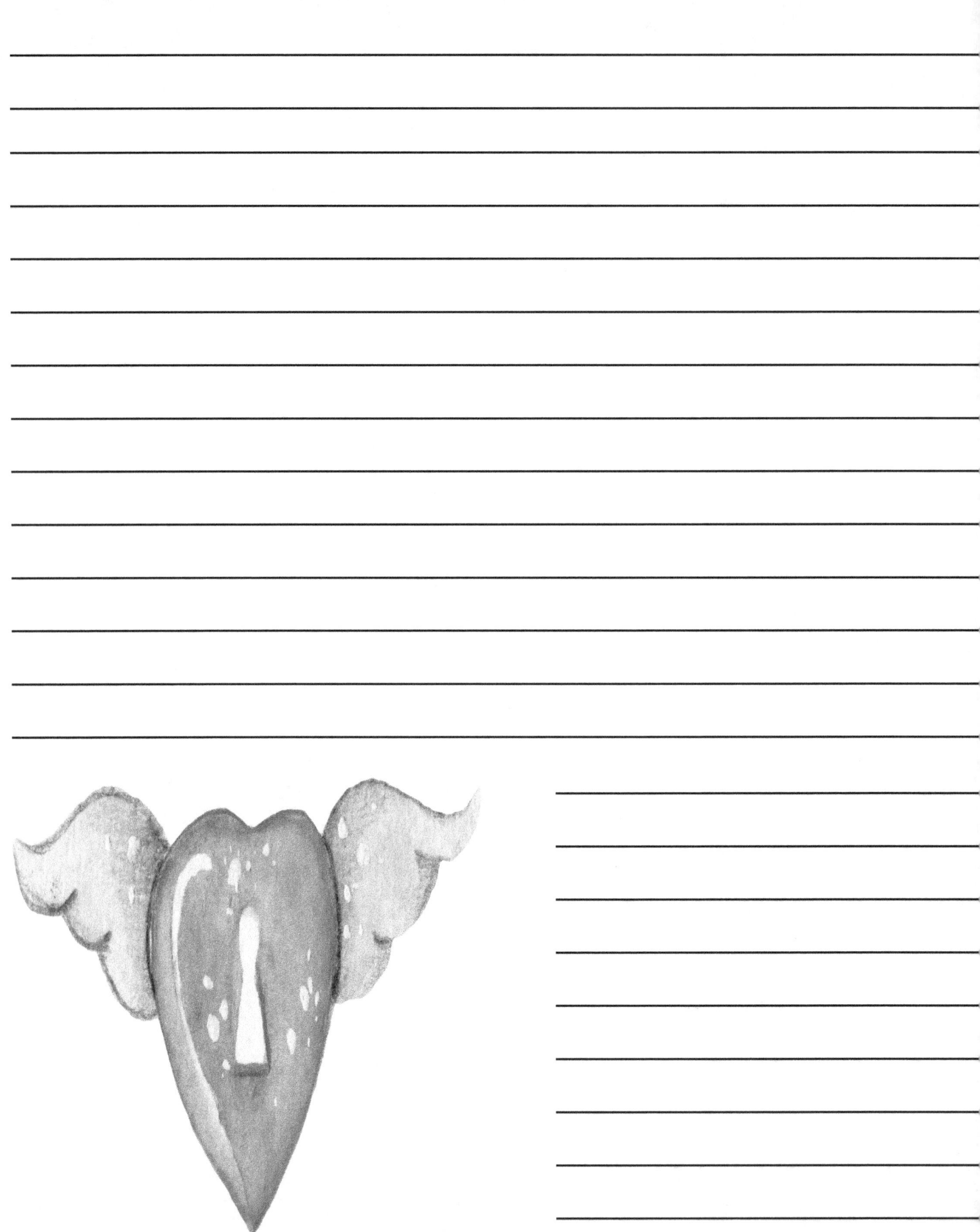

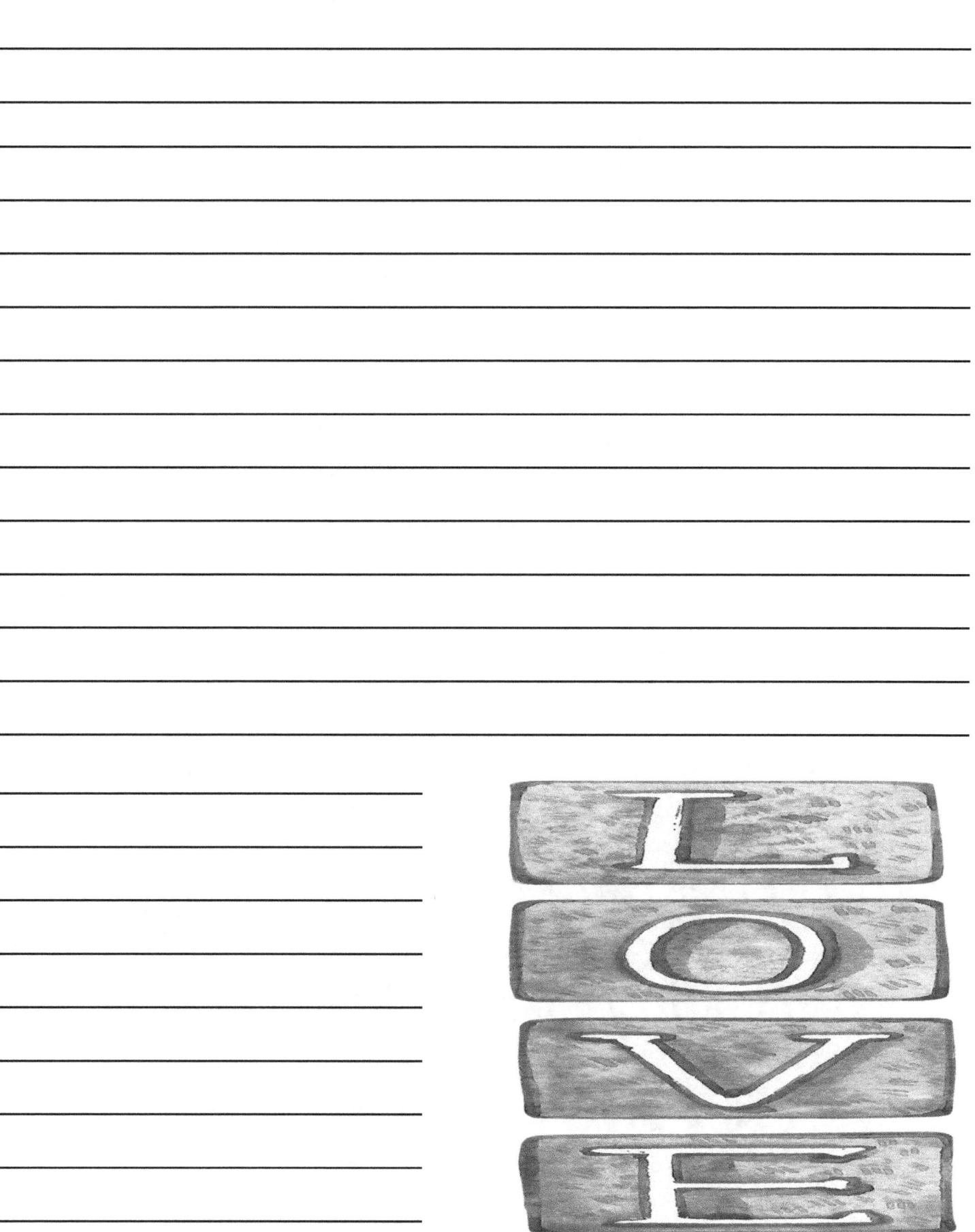

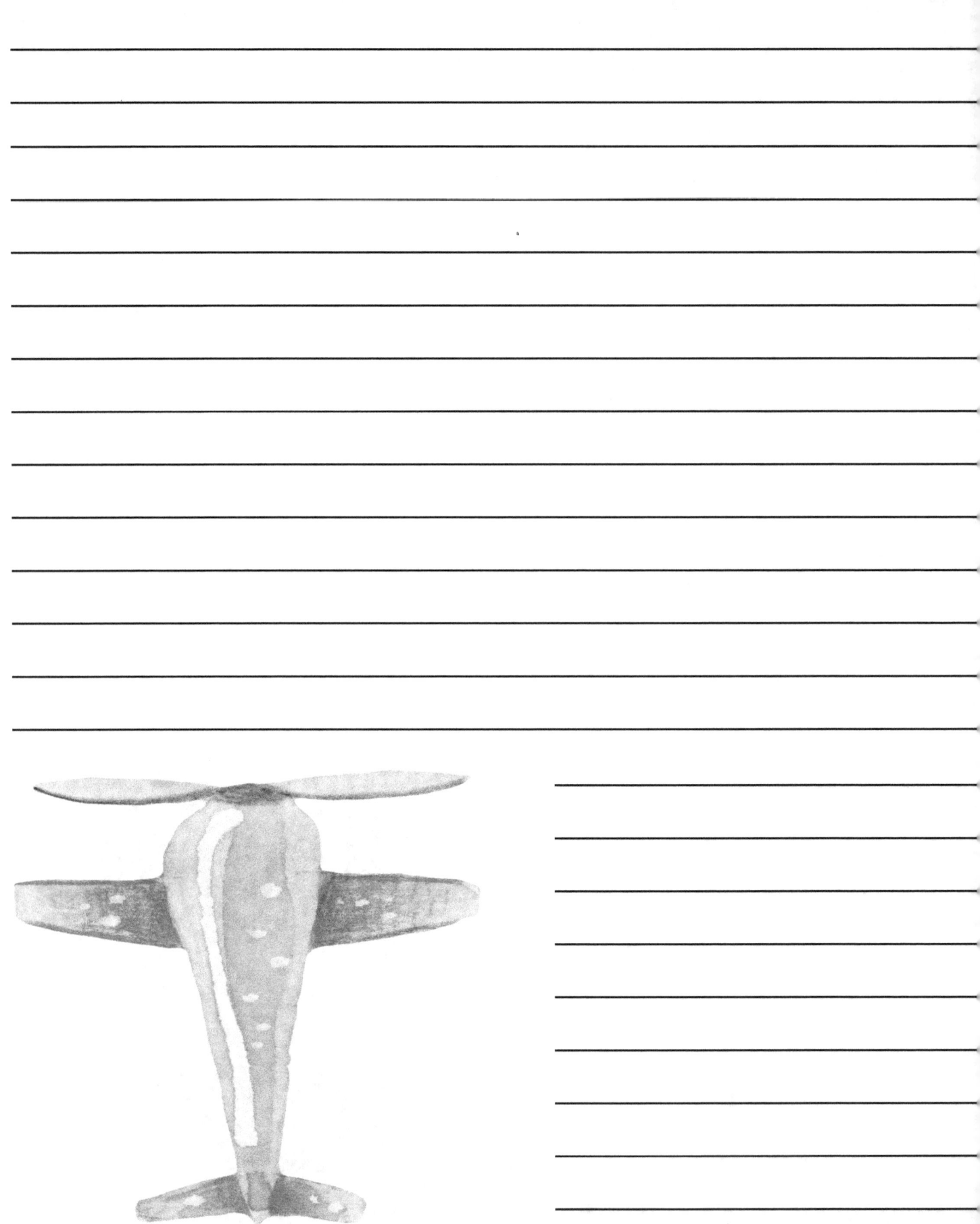

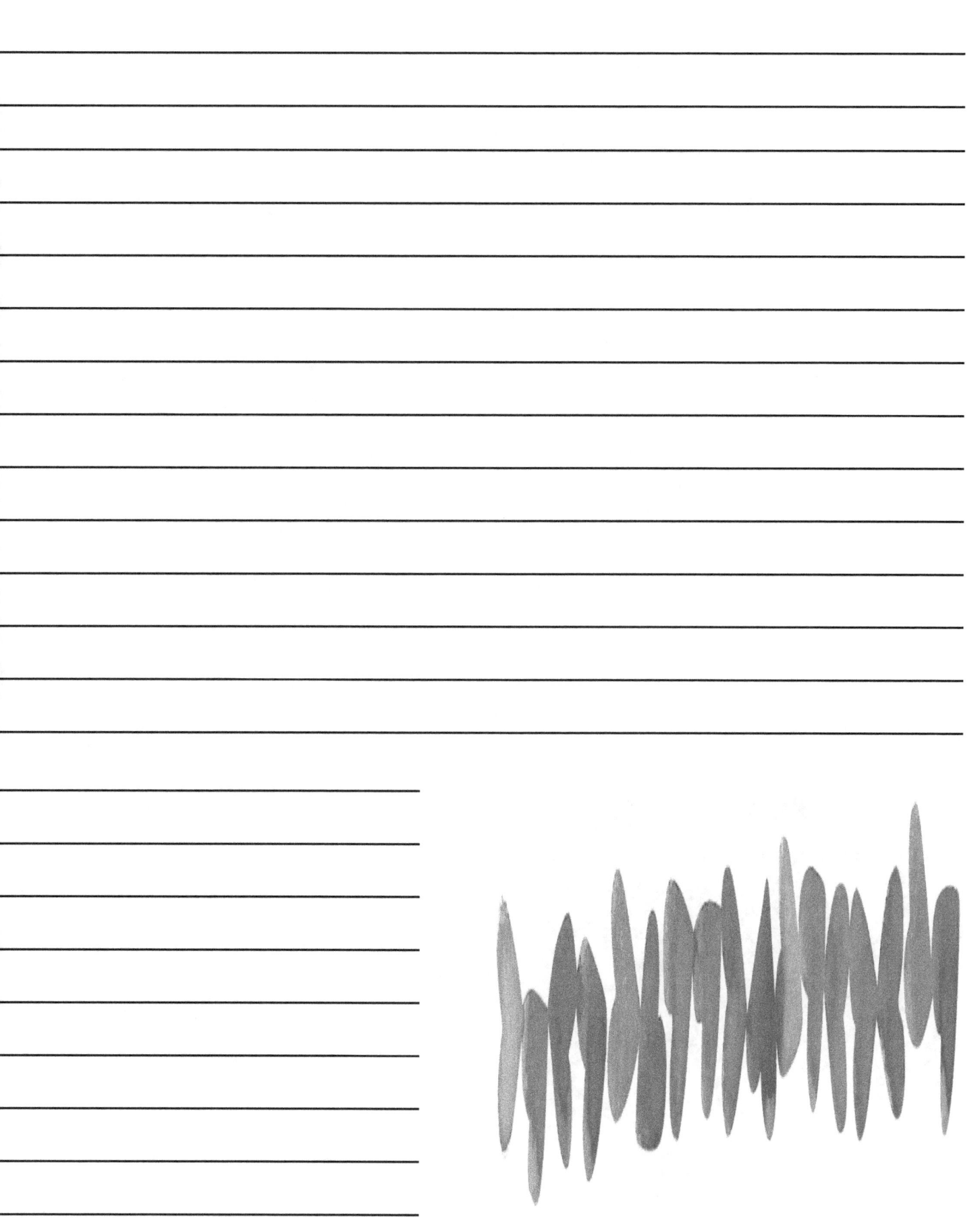

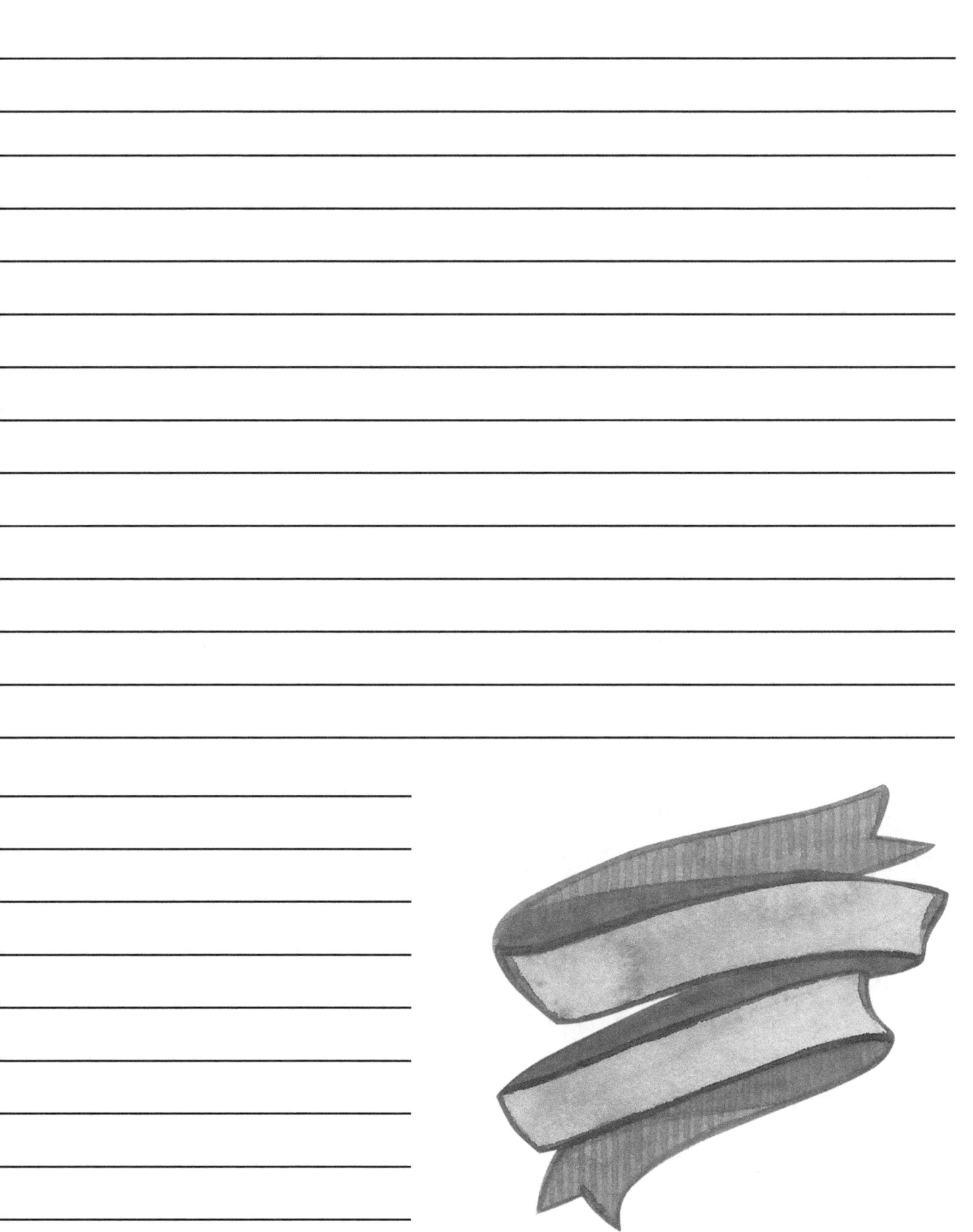

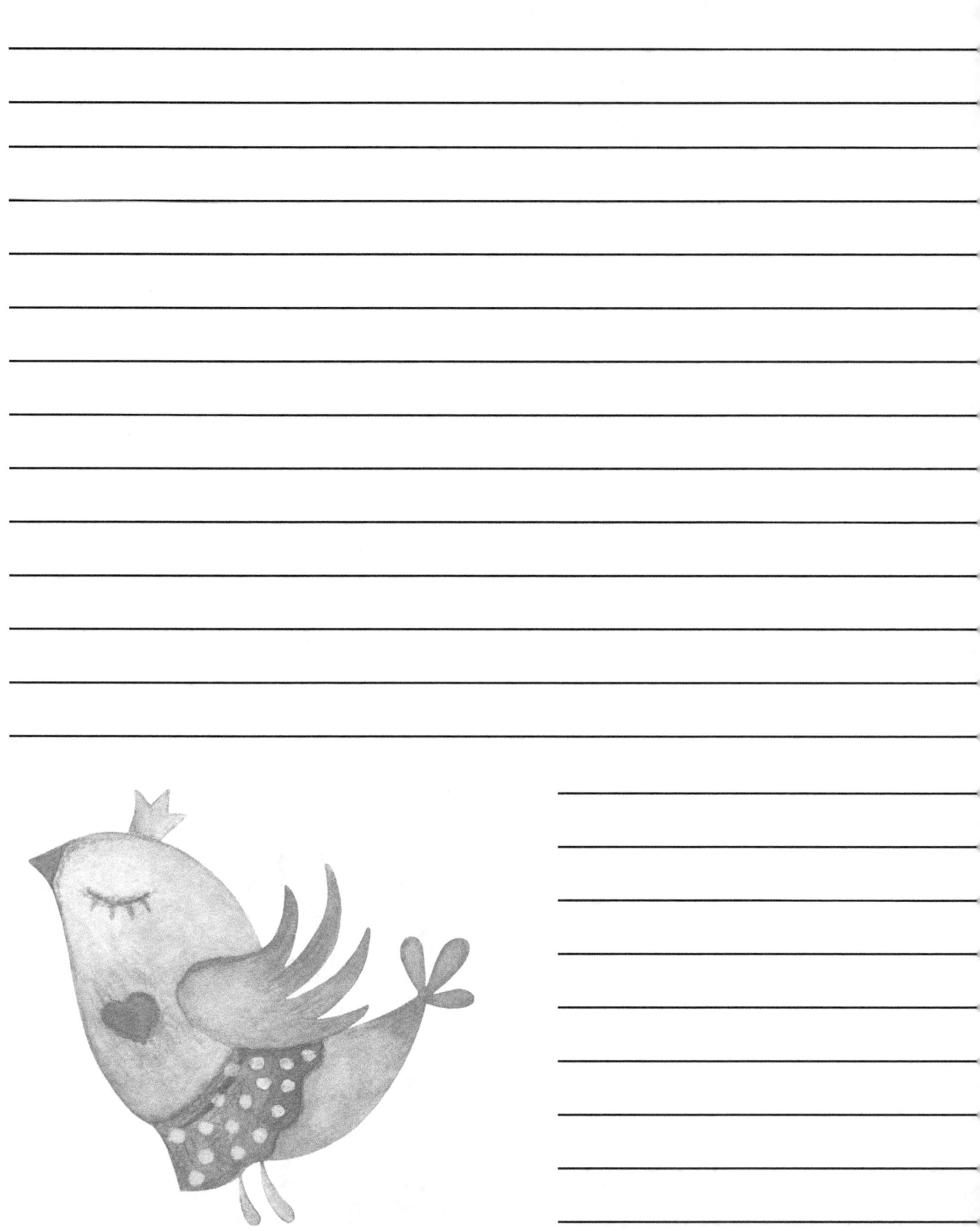

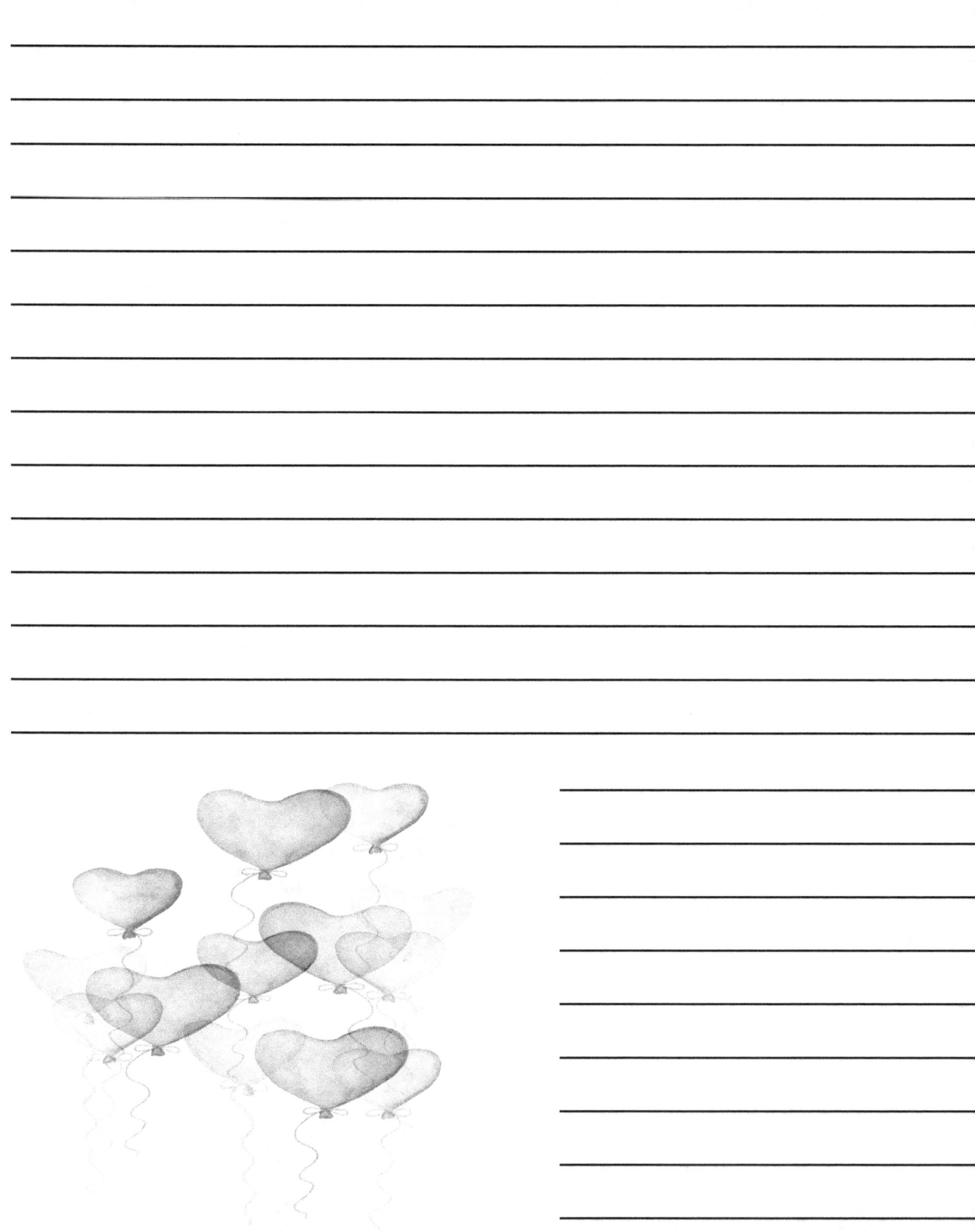

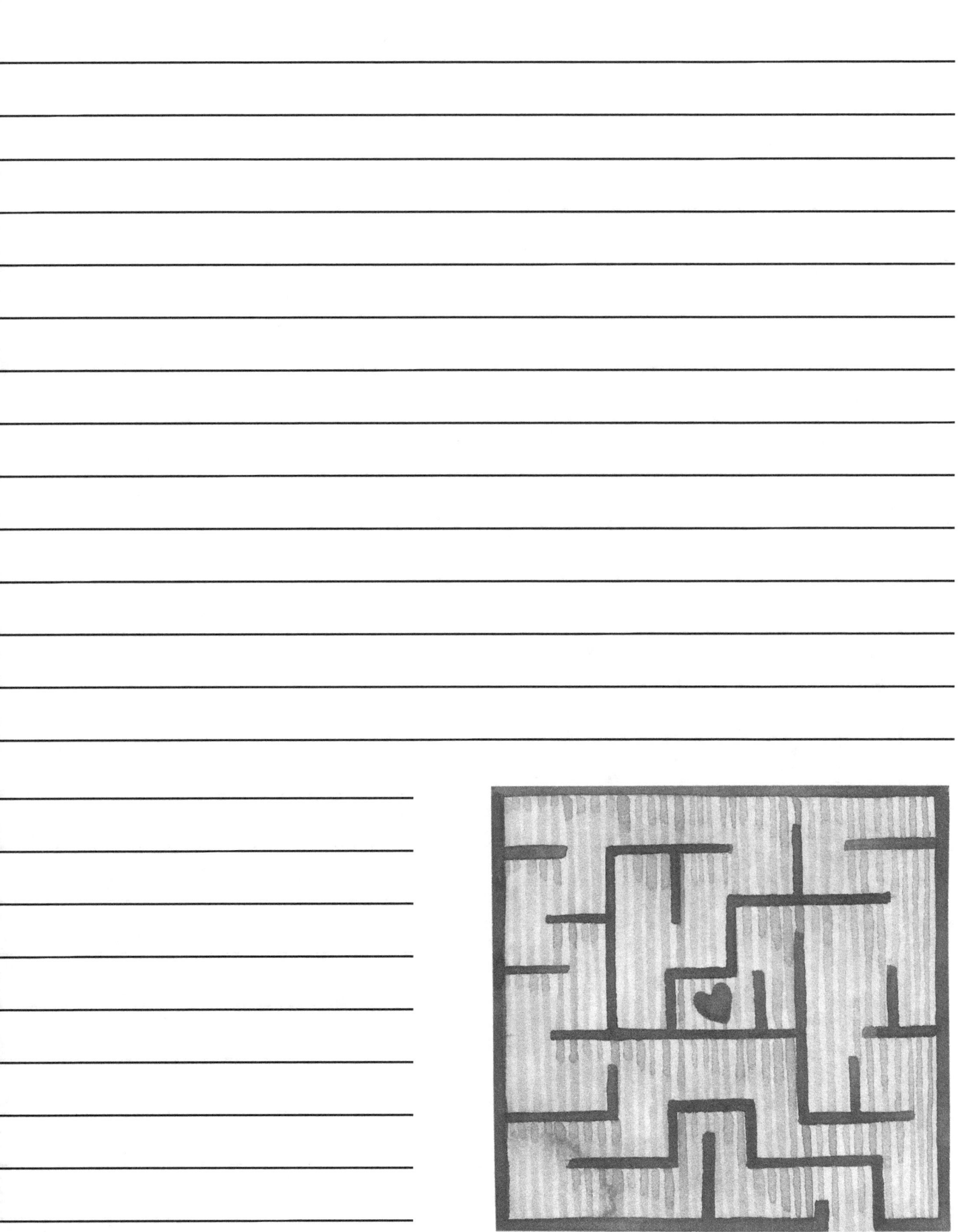

- Acts of Kindness Tracker -

- Acts of Kindness Tracker -

- Acts of Kindness Tracker -

Notes

Notes

Notes

www.ingramcontent.com/pod-product-compliance
Lightning Source LLC
LaVergne TN
LVHW060140080526
838202LV00049B/4035